THE Resurrection

Isaiah 53:4–6 and Matthew 21:1–11; 26;
27:27–66; 28:1–10 for Children

Written by Cynda Strong
Illustrated by Helen Cann

CONCORDIA PUBLISHING HOUSE · SAINT LOUIS

Isaiah's message had foretold
How Christ would save all men:
He'd take upon Himself our sins;
He'd die and rise again.

And so His time on earth did pass,
And many friends did gain,
For He became their earthly lord;
They thought on earth He'd reign.

With palms and garments spread before,
Without a crown of gold,
Our Lord went to Jerusalem
And on a donkey rode.

In parables He taught them all
To live their lives on earth,
To know salvation's gift from God,
The gift of greatest worth.

And Judas, one of Jesus' friends,
Told priests what Jesus claimed.
Denying Him for payment gold,
"Betrayer" he was named.

And so the Twelve made plans to meet,
The Passover was near.
A final meal with Christ they'd eat;
His lessons they would hear.

And at this final meal, our Lord
Served them the wine and bread.
"This is My body and My blood,"
To them our Savior said.

Foes led Him to the priests one day
With questions of His claims.
The priests could find no witnesses,
No one to give Him blame.

To Pilate's seat they took our Lord.
Though Pilate found no wrong,
He sentenced Him to die that day,
His suff'ring would be long.

Upon His head they placed a crown
Of thorns to mock His name.
They spat and yelled and struck His head,
Denouncing Jesus' claim.

They placed Him high upon a cross
And pierced His side with spear.
They placed a sign above His head,
And loudly they did jeer.

The sky turned dark when Jesus died;
He suffered with great pain.
He bore the sins of all that day,
Our home in heav'n to gain.

Then three days passed and Sunday came;
His friends went to His tomb.
But when the women went inside,
They saw that He was gone.

The angels sang with joy that day;
No longer was Christ dead.
He'd conquered sin and death for us,
Just as God's Word had said!

Then joyful praise to God in heav'n,
Like angels we can sing.
For Christ has risen from the dead,
Our Savior and our King!

Dear Parents,

Centuries before the birth of Christ, the prophet Isaiah told not only of His birth but also of His death. With Christ's birth, the fulfillment of the prophecy of God's plan for our salvation began.

Christ grew into manhood, preached, and taught among the people. They watched Him perform miracles, heal the sick, and give hope to the oppressed.

At the end of His three-year ministry, Christ began His journey that would end with His death on the cross. He rode into Jerusalem on the back of a young donkey on the day we celebrate as Palm Sunday—not exactly the triumphant royal entry the people had expected. But Jesus was not meant to be a king on earth.

During those next days, He dined with His faithful followers and encouraged them to keep their faith. He presented the meal we call the Lord's Supper. He was betrayed by one of His faithful and suffered the emotional anguish of being abandoned by God.

As you read the Easter story to your child, he will see the reason we can sing "Alleluia" with the angels. The stone was rolled away. The tomb was empty. Jesus has risen. Now we are assured of our salvation.

Alleluia! He lives!

The Author